Boxer
THE FIGHT WITHIN

NAUSICAA TWILA

Printed in the United States of America

First Printing, 2018

ISBN-13: 978-1719581950

ISBN-10: 1719581959

www.TakingMyMagicBack.com

*For all the fighters
who have inspired me,
and all the fighters
who have allowed me
to inspire them...
THIS IS FOR YOU.*

THE 6 G'S OF
OVERCOMING THE ODDS

GRIT – *Page 5*
The ability to dig in and get the job done.

GRIND – *Page 11*
The day to day routine and constant
progress you love to hate.

GREATNESS – *Page 17*
There is only one person you are competing
with: who you were yesterday.

GLORY – *Page 27*
Glory comes to those who are humble and
give back as a practice and daily effort.

GIVE'ER – *Page 35*
(Canadian Slang) When you've got nothing
left, you dig in, and give a little more.

GROUNDING – *Page 43*
Before you move, find your footing.
Sometimes that means take a rest.

MAGIC – *Page 53*
When you've done all you can do,
leave it to to make up the rest.

B O X E R

You will get hit with the hard stuff. And what seemed hard before, will seem like nothing. You will be stuck. You will wonder if you will survive. You will crawl, you will cry. You will ask yourself if you are dreaming. One day, you will go for a long drive on a road you've never driven before. You will take that medicine, and it will fix nothing. But, you will suddenly become aware of a vastness within you, that will never fold. You will laugh to the sky, tears streaming down your face. There will be no words, no description, no resolution; just silent knowing. From that moment on, when the hard stuff hits, you will bob and weave.

A L W A Y S   N E W

I've been laying low.

Spending time in the lab.

Working hard,

Refining the details.

Pushing through the ugly parts.

Saying to myself:

> *"I'm not done yet. I'm never*
> *done, and I'm always new."* .

F I R S T   P U N C H

When I realized that life would be a fight and that my
angels would sometimes be my ringside coaches, I
jammed my mouth guard into my teeth, bit down hard,
and told life to throw the first punch.

<u>C H E S S   F O R   T H E   G O D S</u>

"You brought it all on yourself..."

Don't fall for that manipulation tactic.

Shit happens to all of us, and most of it is beyond our understanding and ability to control. We control our mind, our behavior and actions.

All else is chess for the gods.

2

W H A T ' S   N E W   W I T H   Y O U ?

I have been busy with life. I have been busy with
Nothing at all. I've been lost, counting the steps I took
since I last knew where I was. I know where I've been--
the memories sting, then pass then swallow me
whole. I've been trying to get up from this position,
I've been trying to make a lasting difference. Can you
hold me up? My arms are scarred, legs about to give
out, I've been holding this world up for longer than my
memory can find me. I am still dreaming. Busy with
goals. Exhausted by wishes, devoured by maybes. I'm
a little dangerous, because I wear a smile, even now.

So, what's new with you?

LOOKING FOR
WAYS TO HANG ON

Don't despair—*There are infinite reasons.* Collect them. Pile them around the empty corners of your mind. Because "hang on" is just the beginning; you cannot build a life on "hang on". You must thrive. This goal may seem out of reach, but listen, you must build a practice, a skill of it. It will take daily effort. You won't feel the results for sometime. It will feel more like chaos than progress, but as you cement your way to a life worth living, you will see that life is not a passive ordeal. Yes—It passes like trains and like dreams. But, you can make of it what you want. Just find those hidden wishes in your mind's abandoned warehouse and decorate your world with everything beautiful and real.

WHAT YOU'RE MADE OF

You know that feeling you got when they made you
feel worthless like you were nothing?

Hold onto it.

It will be worth something when you finally show them
what you are actually made of.

HELL + BACK

I've been to hell and back a thousand times
since we last spoke. I still wear the same smile,
but this time, the shine in my eyes is spiked
with a luminous void you'd call depth.

3

GREATNESS

B E S T   O F   U S

We climbed the moon with proof of our existence clenched in our depths. They told us to hit the road, that they had nothing for us, and we walked barefoot all night. We laughed into the sky, we never felt so free. They came looking for us after that, but all they found was an old, worn suitcase they deemed worthless. They threw it to the beasts of the night who ripped it to shreds across the darkened sky. The best of us lives on like stars.

HIGH CONTRAST

There's a quality to those people who grew up truly loved. It's this unshakable confidence. A certain smile, a flow of emotion. An unquestioning ability. It is stunning. Tragedies come and go but they never include...not being loved... For those who went unloved, because of some event--either real or interpreted—in childhood...they have...crooked smiles... Shaky voices...An inability to express out the beauty they hold within.

They have a special kind of beauty.

They are like high contrast images, sharply defined by the darkness they hold within. Colors are more intense. Mood: more mysterious... And if they light a candle deep inside their soul, that self-ignited flame will carry them...*forever.*

ENJOY THE FIGHT

Enjoy life. For some of us that means enjoy the fight, because life is a fight. From the moment we are born we are fighting for a chance to continue on, to endure. That doesn't have to be a bad thing if you can sink into it and feel alive from it. Fight for your life, you are worth it. Do you realize how many miracles it took to lead you to this living breathing moment? Capture it. Fight for it. You have come this far; *that is greatness.*

A DIFFERNT KIND OF BEAUTIFUL

She's another kind of beauty--

wild hair,

Blunt tongue

kind of beauty.

Unboxed kind of beauty.

Never ending adventure

kind of beauty.

she is a different

kind of beautiful.

G R O W   W I T H   M E

Grow with me.

Leave the past behind.

Be brave.

Grow where you feel broken.

Grow where you feel small.

Grow where you feel burdened.

Be brave with me.

Don't count the mistakes.

Count how many things you want to do.

List them.

Unravel them.

Grow a path to them.

Grow.

Don't be afraid.

All your guardians are watching.

And they are filling in the cracks.

So keep on moving.

Towards the sky,

Up,

Up,

Up...

KNOCKED DOWN
THE KNOCK DOWN

She got up,

Got knocked down,

Got up,

Got knocked down,

Got up,

Got knocked down,

Until one day,

She decided to get up

With so much fury and determination

That she *knocked down the knock down.*

A V A N T - G A R D E   E L E G A N C E

she was never the same again. and it was never clear
whether this was true because of her own insecurities
or others'. one day, she will be sure of herself again;
she will embrace her differences with her very own
brand of *avant-garde elegance.*

HIDDEN TREASURE

I can't lead you back to yourself anymore than I can find hidden treasure in an unknown land with no map. You know this land and you must map your treasure. As I find my own treasure, it will remind you and encourage your journey. But the hidden realms you must explore are yours alone. That's the adventure, the beauty, the journey. You are yours to discover.

4

F O U L   P L A Y

When you pulled out your blade, you thought no one was looking, and you aimed directly for my heart. While observing your perfect timing and precision, it was clear to me that you had done this before. I looked into your eyes, smiled and even offered you a place at my table. I see what you are. Your mask came off. And my heart is fine; *you missed.*

Y O U   W I L L   G O   F A R

You will go far;
Far beyond these guttered dreams and half empty
glasses. You will find your pace through inspirations
and brilliant revelations. They will come to you as you
follow the still, small voice inside. You will get a flash
of bravery, you will act on it and nothing will ever be
the same. You will create life with your beautiful mind.
Starting right now. *Lasting forever.*

FOR R.S. WILIAMS

MANY GATES

I have many gates in my castle. Many hallways to roam. Many doors, bolted shut. Everyone is welcome in my courtyard, but my gates within are designed in layers to keep loveless hearts out. There are no keys, but only those who dream deeply and endlessly are allowed in.

A D V E N T U R E

She struggled too much, likely more than she needed
to, but this struggle awakened her heart and her fight.
It made her passion come alive, and taught her how to
smile in the face of challenges. In time, she learned to
struggle without suffering, and it became less of a
struggle and more of an adventure that exhilarated
her heart and mind.

THE FIGHT

I am fighting. i have been fighting. i know you have
been too. i have been knocked down, displaced,
unconscious. I woke up lost. I couldn't remember
what i was fighting for anymore. My fists kept
swinging, at the world, at myself. I wanted to stay
down, i wanted to stay lost. i raged at the savagery of
it all. i raged because fighting was all i had left. i woke
up alone. The tears re-calibrated my body. I found
something unshakable within. It was never about the
fight. It was about something more. I retired my
boxing gloves for my scarred bare hands. Sometimes
the fight is won by not fighting anymore.

Sometimes the fight is won by not fighting anymore.

E X T R E M E   S P O R T

This life

is an extreme sport;

you have to train,

get in the zone,

and most importantly,

NEVER GIVE UP.

I ROSE AGAIN

I fell

I crashed

I broke

I cried

I crawled

I hurt

I surrendered

and then...

I ROSE AGAIN.

<u>A N Y T H I N G</u>

Anything that fucks up your flow.

Anything that leaves you breathless and alone.

Anything that punches you in the gut.

Anything that puts you in a rut.

Anything you can't do.

Anything that unleashes darkness in your heart...

USE IT.

Find the everything in your soul that is stronger than
the anything that's beating you down, and be the first
to wrestle it to the ground, every time.

H A N G I N G

I hung in there, like those blue tides that
wrapped around my ankles and swung me
from the edge of the moon.
I was the hero, the muse, and the lost
dreamer. I was strength which felt more
like weakness pushed past its absolute limits.

B R E A K   T H E   M O L D

I saw that I could finish this race on my own, without compromising my soul in any way, and that's when I felt my body filled with a power I cannot describe. I sprinted like I never knew I could. That is growth; your body finally being allowed to break it's mold held by the mind.

GROUNDING

GOOD THINGS
BLOOM IN OBSCURITY

Did you ever realize how hard the fight for existence can become? It can be dehumanizing, raw, overloaded with anguish and pain. It can make a good soul turn cruel and a wise soul do foolish things, and a pure soul become jaded. It's not just dark, It's bitterly cold. It feels like death. It feels final. Like there is no way out... This is where most souls give up. They take this darkness, chew it and swallow it. They believe in the horrors of life, and those horrors paralyze them. But there is a time to rest and a time to fight. When death's icy grip lands upon your shoulder, you better show him what you're worth. That's how good things bloom in obscurity.

S T I L L   B E A U T I F U L

I will

deal with

it privately.

I will find my footing.

I will go within. I will

connect to my inner

resources. Because

I know that life is

still beautiful.

<u>S H A R P E R</u>

I will never
get thick skin.
I prefer to sharpen
my edges.

_H O W_

I won't ask the usual questions of myself.
I will only ask myself this:

_How do I drop this world off my shoulders and use my
senses to navigate the present reality?_
Who am I?
Where do I want to go?
How can I function effectively?

Make no mistake--this is an adventure.

How do I breathe?
How do I navigate?
How do I live?

PEOPLE WANT THINGS

Everyone wants something.

Some fight hard to bend the world to their will. Some follow crowds and trends and cues as to what to do next. Some read the opinion section to learn what their opinion should be. And some, very few, unplug from it all to want nothing, be nothing and think nothing. *These no-minds are the most powerful of all.*

<u>O W N   D A M N   S E L F</u>

she was soft

like hell and

dark like black ice

she left branding

to the hustlers

she was her

own damn self

H O M E C O M I N G

I have lived long enough to realize I cant ever ask
anything of anyone. And that my pain may never be
understood. And, those who care will be absent
minded to what really comforts you. Also, when life
hurts, it means you've ventured too far out of yourself.
Call your soul home. Because that homecoming will
be all you need. *You'll see.*

B I G G E R   P I C T U R E

Maybe you're not seeing the bigger picture.

Maybe there is more, yet unseen. Yes, you can step back and take in a panoramic view. But, tell me, what is beyond that horizon? It's a feeling, it's a wish, it's something not yet perceivable. Maybe you can't see it all quite yet. Maybe that's OK.

Sometimes the vision comes by intuition alone...

IMAGINE

I believe you have
a powerful enough
mind that you will
damn well imagine
things into existence.

S H E   C A M E   B A C K

She came back, *but she came back changed.*

She smiled a little tighter, eyes, a little darker, like someone hit the dim switch. She was candlelight, when she used to be the sun, a lost stranger, when she used to be a long lost friend. I wanted to pick her up in my arms and tell her that it was OK; that she was jaded now and that I loved her this way too. It's true—I missed her carefree smile, but I wanted to know the darkened girl before me, *more.*

_L O O K_

If you find yourself on the quiet part of town
where eyes don't recognize each other and
freedom comes with a price, just remember
that the windows are always unlocked and
that brick wall dead-end is a curtain.

_L O O K   B E H I N D   I T._

<u>O N C E   I N   A   W H I L E</u>

every once in a while

i remember how

you painted my skies purple

and how you made

the ghetto look beautiful

and how we almost said forever...

i know you are waiting for me

under some purple sky

but i cannot tell

if we are meant for this life

or the next

either way

the adventure we traveled

will spell our names

across the earth

every night

between the

sun,

moon

and stars.

B U R N I N G ; _A L I V E_

I'm on the edge of

creating something great,

I am in the verge of tearing down boxed in thinking,

I am nowhere,

I am everywhere,

I am burning; alive.

THE HAUNTING

there are memories I keep
      that keep me
      breathless and surreal
      not of my mind
      but of my whole being--
      awakening to
      the original ghost i am
      as i haunt this vessel
      this home
      this body.

S U R V I V O R - S A G E

I am a survivor and a sage.
All things thrown at me
will light my path and turn
to ashes under my feet.

THE UNIVERSE IS MAGIC

Have your own back.

The universe is magic and will support you when you
are on the right path. Don't worry about small minds
and shallow souls. They have a different home.

T H O U G H T   P A I N T I N G S

What if your pain

was simply thoughts

painted upon you,

would you peel it off

and declare yourself *new?*

_K A L I_

I changed my name a thousand times
 and burned my skin to remove the memories.
They are gone from my body but they are all around
me. I'm out of gasoline and my feet are numb.
I will make things beautiful.
That will be my destruction.

YOU ARE THE UNIVERSE

Don't surrender your worth.

Surrender everything else, but keep your worth tucked
away in a secret part of your heart. Let the waves
come. Let them crash down—they won't hurt you. Let
the flames come. Let them burn up your world, into a
brilliant light show. Throw your past into the wind, let
it remind you of your spirit.

Brave, bright soul—

surrender, *surrender.*
    Unfold, *unfold.*
        You should know: *You are the universe.*

FOR SHIANNA

Boxer

A B O U T   T H E   A U T H O R

Hello, my name is Nausicaa Twila. I am an poet and independent author of 10 books. I use writing as a tool for healing and self expression and encourage others to do the same. In redefining my reality using words, I find incredible self-empowerment and the realization that all the answers, truly are, within. If a mindset can color your world as a prison or a wonderful haven, why not tap into those tools? This book is about finding the fight to exist or go on when one feels hopeless. Finding the tools to fight back, not with the other, but with your own inner stagnancy. We can, all of us, become great when we remember the competition is only with who we happened to be yesterday.

My books are all available on Amazon.com:

1. *Beautiful Minds Anonymous (a book of poems)*
2. *Beautiful Minds Anonymous II (burner of ships)*
3. *Beautiful Minds Anonymous III (mythical creatures)*
4. *Chronicles From Another Reality*
5. *Overcoming Journal*
6. *The Sweetest Goodbye*
7. *Soledad*
8. *Taking My Magic Back*
9. *Home*
10. *BOXER*

C O N N E C T

NausicaaTwila@Gmail.com

Instagram.com/NausicaaTwila

wwww.TakingMyMagicBack.com

NOTES & DREAMS

31940568R00055

Printed in Great Britain
by Amazon